THE
LIFE
OF A
Lab

There is sorrow enough in the natural way

From men and women to fill our day;

But when we are certain of sorrow in store,

Why do we always arrange for more?

Brothers and sisters, I bid you beware

Of giving your heart to a dog to tear.

Rudyard Kipling,
from "The Power of the Dog"

THE
LIFE
OF A
Lab

Text by E. Donnall Thomas Jr.

Photography by Denver Bryan

Ducks Unlimited, Inc.
Memphis, Tennessee
1999

and

Willow Creek Press
Minocqua, Wisconsin
1999

Photographer: Denver Bryan
Author: E. Donnall Thomas Jr.

Editor: Chuck Petrie
Photography editor: Diane Jolie
Book Design: Dit Rutland
Asst. Book Design: Monte Clair Finch

Published by Ducks Unlimited, Inc.

Julius Wall, President
Gene Henry, Chairman of the Board
Matthew B. Connolly, Jr., Executive Vice President
Chris Dorsey, Group Manager of Publishing and Communications

ISBN   1-57223-265-X

Published April 1999

Printed in Canada

Library of Congress Cataloging-in-Publication Data

Thomas, E. Donnall.
    The life of a lab / text by E. Donnall Thomas, Jr. ;
photography by Denver Bryan ; [editor, Chuck Petrie].
        p. cm.
    ISBN 1-57223-265-X [hc.]
    1. Labrador retriever. 2. Labrador retriever Pictorial
works. I. Bryan, Denver. II. Petrie, Chuck III. Title.
SF429.L3T48 1999
636.752 í 7--dc21
                                                99-25187
                                                       CIP

AUTHOR'S ACKNOWLEDGEMENTS

The author wishes to express his gratitude to West Wind's Sunrise and Skykomish Sunka Zee, without whom the creation of this text would not have been possible.

PHOTOGRAPHER'S ACKNOWLEDGEMENTS

For my mother, Darlene…a true believer

This book would not have been possible without the help of many people. First and foremost among them are Eric and Marc Pierce of Bozeman, Montana. This father and son team, in business (Big Sky Carvers) and in recreation, have generously subjected themselves, their families and their Labs to my frequently probing cameras. For this I am very thankful.

I would also like to thank my publishers, Duck's Unlimited and Willow Creek Press, for their support throughout. The unwavering commitment to excellence of my editor, Chuck Petrie, as well as the talents of photo editor, Diane Jolie, were in no small part responsible for this book's final form.

Other friends and acquaintances who have graciously allowed me the opportunity to photograph the "other member" of their family (dog's names are italicized) include Heather Andrews and *Sage*; Pete, Tanya, Ty and Q Rothing of Diamond R Kennels in Bozeman, Montana; Jason Wise and Sarah Pittack and *Teal*; Shari, Bridger, Teal, Jackson and Jade Pierce and *Chance* and *Madison*; Jared Brown and Steve Wilburn and *Champ*; Brian, Jenny, and Mackenzie Grossenbacher and *Maddie* and *Ray*; Kim Leighton and *Sam*; Mark and Diane Thibeault and *Abby*; Dave Carson and *Mac*; Susan Blackwood and *Sasha*; Dave Corchoran and *Molly*; Mike and Diane Atwell and *Bridger*; Leonard Houser of Thunder Ridge Kennels in Billings, Montana; John and Laurel Berger and *Honey* and *Katie*; Greg, Kirsten and Madison Hoell and *Beau*; Carter Walker and *Indy*; Nate Jorgenson and *Nellie*; Joby Sabol and *Moose*; Cindy Younkin and *Buck*; Lisa Flood and *Moose*; Jim Klug and *Bo*; Tom and Linda Roffe and *Dillon*; Rod and Pam King and *Ace*; Julia Myers and *Tucker*; Jeff Lawrence and *Montana*; Nels Nelson and *Abe*; Craig, Connie and Carver Bergstedt and *Lockie*; Ken Vandewalle and *Jake* and *Val*; Kathy Rogers and *Woody*; Margo Page and *Petie*; Bayless, Stacy and Keaton Ward and *Abby*; Gary Behrent and *Zooey*; Sam and Chris Cunningham and *Jackson*; Bob Sobretena and *Bo*; Kristin and Daniel Harding and *Max*; John Borchert and *Chessie*; Larry McMurry and *Pepper*; Dana Giovannello and *Cooper*; Tom Fritz and *Ema*; Ty Bergien and *Bahgeera*; Mitch Bubholtz and *Sam*; Al, Christine and Jake Dunayer and *Goldie*; Dave Cook and *Ranger*; Andrew and Gabrielle West; Danielle Thompson; Amy Branson; Lauren and Connor Brown; Don, Maggie, Mia and Beau Banducci; and, last but not least, Anne Sexton.

DUCKS UNLIMITED, INC.

The mission of Ducks Unlimited is to fulfill the annual life cycle needs of North American waterfowl by protecting, enhancing, restoring and managing important wetlands and associated uplands. Since its founding in 1937, DU has raised more than $1.3 billion, which has contributed to the conservation of over 8.2 million acres of prime wildlife habitat in all fifty states, each of the Canadian provinces and in key areas of Mexico. In the U.S. alone, DU has helped to conserve more than 1.3 million acres of waterfowl habitat. Some 900 species of wildlife live and flourish on DU projects, including many threatened or endangered species.

Table of Contents

THE LIFE OF A LAB

Introduction

Encapsulating all the elements that quantify the life of a Labrador retriever, especially in a single book, is a daunting task. Daunting because every Lab is singular in the eyes of its master or mistress, imbued with individual character, unique virtues and, let's admit it, the individual faults and foibles that define any dog.

Individuality aside, at least for the moment, Labs collectively come in three basic colors-black, yellow, and chocolate. And even though they may have countless personalities, they share a pleasant, easy-going temperament that makes them the most popular breed of retriever in the world. They are certainly the most popular breed of retriever in America.

I know this not only because the number of American Kennel Club registrations for the breed say it is so, but because many members of Ducks Unlimited are retriever owners, and the vast majority of them own, or are owned by, Labrador retrievers (often more than one at a time). Over the years, I've had the opportunity to spend countless enjoyable hours in the hunting clubs, goose pits, duck blinds, and homes of more than a few of these men and women, and, usually, their Labs have been constantly at their side.

Life with Labs: Nurturing them as puppies, training them as young dogs, polishing their skills as mature Labs, and doting over them in their old age are ways we affect their quality of

life and mold relationships with them. Over a Lab's lifetime, the relationship between dog and master or mistress often becomes something special, memorable. I've seen those bonds develop many times, and know of them, too, from the tributes and eulogies–letters, stories, and even book-length manuscripts–we receive at Ducks Unlimited when our members' beloved Lab partners are gone. These memorials are genuine, heart wrenching, and they reveal the depth of affection people feel for their canine companions, who in many cases were also their best friends.

Of course, many Labs and their owners are not hunters, and there is certainly nothing wrong with that. After all, this versatile breed of dog is commonly employed in other occupa-

tions, including guide dog to the visually impaired, rescue dog, sentry dog, war dog, drug detection dog, and therapy dog, among others. Thus, while it would be impossible to encapsulate in this book the life of any single Lab, photographer Denver Bryan and author E. Donnall Thomas Jr. have combined their talents to capture the common essence, that spirit that personifies the lives of all members of this fascinating breed. Here is a word-and-picture story that anyone who has ever owned a Lab will enjoy, one that will evoke reminiscences of their own Labs, whether those dogs are alive today or are living on as cherished memories.

—*Matthew B. Connolly, Jr.*
Executive Vice President,
Ducks Unlimited, Inc.

Preface

It is now official, according to the American Kennel Club. The Labrador retriever is the most popular dog in America. That's quite an accomplishment for a breed originally developed to fulfill one of the narrowest canine job descriptions imaginable: recovering downed ducks from icy water. It should be obvious that many of today's Lab enthusiasts have no intention of employing their dogs for such a purpose, which can be cause for either celebration or despair depending on one's point of view. In either case, these curious facts demand an explanation. How did a breed designed for such an obscure purpose win so many hearts along the way?

The answer involves no small amount of serendipity. There is no apparent reason why the character traits necessary to motivate a dog to enter a cold ocean should inspire affection, as demonstrated by the Lab's comparatively surly cohort, the Chesapeake Bay retriever. But somehow Labs turned out differently, with personalities that border on the irresistible. Even those who ask a lot of their dogs in the field recognize that they aren't just dealing with hunting machines. They are dealing with friends and members of the family.

Lab people tend to define the stages of their own lives by their dogs, just as ordinary civilians mark them by the growth and development of their children. It can be disorienting to realize how much life an eager dog can pack into a mere dozen years, especially as those years come to a close. And that is the theme underlying this book. Like all good stories, Labs come with a beginning, middle, and end. In word and image, we have tried to capture the magic of this passage and explain the compelling significance it holds for its human participants.

And now, let's hear from the dogs.

—*E. Donnall Thomas Jr., Lewistown, MT*

CHAPTER ONE

Puppyhood

Womb, birth canal, whelping box … by this apparently simple progression, each new Labrador retriever enters a brave new world of all but limitless adventure, not just for the dog but for its owners, handlers, and members of the extended family, and in the best of cases, those fortunate enough to share the pinnacle of the dog's genetic mission in life: the hunt.

However, since Labs remain a product of human hope and expectation, the process of their arrival is actually a bit more complicated than birth itself. The creation of a new Lab often begins well before conception, with careful scrutiny of pedigrees and thoughtful compari-

son of canine virtues, both real and imagined, in potential sires and dams. But it's all a crapshoot in the end, and better odds are the best that carefully chosen bloodlines can offer. Stellar breedings produce their share of pot-lickers, and countless memorable Labs have arrived by accident, the result of a canine desire to procreate that exceeded an owner's diligence. Of course, those matters take years to sort themselves out. In the beginning, they're all just puppies, miniature bundles of energy whose capacity to charm quite properly outweighs all speculation about their future potential.

The first days of a Lab's life belong to the

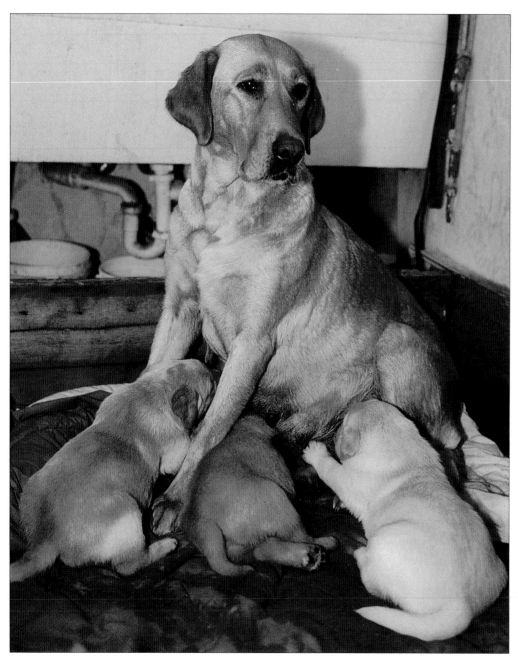

company of littermates and mother. There just isn't much time for anything but nursing, sleeping, and the first blind stirrings of sibling rivalry when it's time to belly up to the chow line. But then a remarkable transformation takes place. As eyes open, coats turn fluffy, and bandy legs gather beneath elusive centers of gravity, real puppies appear as if by magic, and the human impulse to visit the new litter again and again proves all but irresistible.

The optimal way to make one's first real introduction to a new litter comes by way of a sense ordinarily ceded to the dogs themselves: smell. There is simply nothing like the rich, joyous aroma of a dog box full of wiggling Lab puppies. Close your eyes and drink it in. Unrelated adjectives hurtle through the brain like ducks whistling past in the darkness just before dawn: innocent, irresistible, comforting. It's hard to imagine anyone failing to respond

to the appeal of this glorious smell and all the future hope and promise it conveys.

In the beginning, littermates tend to react en masse, like a school of bonefish or a covey of quail. Enter their world to romp with one of them and you will soon find yourself surrounded by them all. But as days pass and the pups continue to grow, individual personalities start to emerge as you bestow secret names on the members of the litter, names that often sound as if they came right out of *Snow White*: Lazy, Grumpy, Sad-Eyes, Noisy, Terror. How those puppy personalities translate into adult behavior traits remains a matter of conjecture, but one point remains indisputable: they're individuals now, not just cloned parts of an organic whole.

Since all the characteristics we love most about Labrador puppies are fundamentally childlike, their inevitable affinity with our own children should come as no surprise. Kids and Lab puppies are drawn together by forces as compelling and mysterious as gravity. They trust one another intuitively and share the secrets of a splendid world we adults once inhabited ourselves but can now return to only by way of memory. What better way to enjoy that vicarious journey than by watching a seven-year-old kid and a seven-week-old Lab explore the lawn together, each an infinite bundle of energy and imagination?

Kids and Lab puppies seem to bring out the best in each other. Perhaps each party recognizes the other's fundamental innocence. Kids playing with puppies never seem to get into any serious trouble, while puppies romping with kids always romp a bit harder than they do in the company of adults, as if childish enthusiasm for life could be passed back and forth between species and amplified in the process.

The bonds that develop between kids and puppies can produce both triumph and despair. If you are picking a new Lab from a litter, watching your child walk back to the car wear-

ing a giddy smile and cradling a slightly nervous puppy can be one of parenthood's defining moments. The puppy will soon become a rival for your own affection, but you can feel confident it will also grow into an unquestioning friend ready to ease the child's own eventual passage through the trials of adolescence. On the other hand, if you are raising the litter, you will have to share the kids' pained silence every time one of the pups heads off to its own new home, and when the family favorite's turn comes round at last, a few tears should be expected. Of course, such gains and losses are an inevitable part of life's algebra, and it's hard to imagine a fairer introduction to this principle than the one a litter of Labs can provide.

The separation from mother and littermates that takes place near the end of the pup's second month marks the first major passage in a young Lab's life. From that moment onward, the world of maternal nurturing recedes forever, replaced by a paradoxical combination of individual independence and growing loyalty to the one person who will serve forever as Boss and Best Friend. For Labs are properly known as one-man dogs, a gender insensitive term that nonetheless accurately describes the breed's relationship to humans, of whom Labs only identify two types: you and all the rest. You may be young or old, male or female, experienced or an utter novice when it comes to the business of training dogs. None of that matters to your

new charge. As far as the pup is concerned, you are the center of the universe, for better or worse. Needless to say, this is not a responsibility to be taken lightly.

The best approach to making friends with a new pup embodies the basic principles of parenting itself: Have as much fun together as you can, set rules gently but firmly, and back everything up with unconditional love, notions that serve well whether the goal is a family pet or a field trial champion. Fortunately, the typical Labrador personality makes all that come easily, especially the parts about the fun and the love. If it were otherwise, Labs would not be the most popular breed of dog in America, no matter how many ducks they retrieve or pheasants they flush.

Of course, there will be trying moments, as in the raising of any youngster. Fortunately, house-breaking comes easily for Labs, and a bit of discouragement after a wayward puddle or two is usually all it takes. Chewing is another matter. There is a world of difference between chewing and biting, and Lab puppies hardly ever stand guilty of the latter. But as a rule of thumb, it's safe to assume that anything within reach is fair game for the young Lab's eager mouth, and if the pup chews anything of value, you really have no one but yourself to blame.

All good Labs deserve an eventual introduction to water, and puppyhood is as good a time as any. Fortunately, Labs take to water as natu-

rally as the ducks they will eventually be called upon to retrieve from it. If you've done your job and exercised those parenting skills properly, the pup should be ready to follow you anywhere. So pick a nice day and wade right in. The pup will scarcely realize that a change of elements has occurred, and in no time the dog will be swimming circles around you. Literally. (If you happen to be fishing at the time, please note that the combination of Lab puppies and fine fly rods is a prescription for disaster.)

At some point during early puppyhood, the young dog will begin to demonstrate the instinct that distinguishes Labs from all those other nice dogs out there: the desire to retrieve. It's a miracle really, for the impulse to mark thrown objects, pick them up, and return them to where they came from cannot be taught in any formal sense. This overriding urge seems especially miraculous when demonstrated in tireless fashion by a dog still small enough to fit in your boot. Of course there will come a time to channel that instinct, but refinement should wait until later. During puppyhood, it's best to accept the young dog's interest as a promise of things still to come.

How much actual training should a young dog receive during its first year of life? Opinions have varied as long as there have been Labs and trainers. Perhaps the best answer is that it depends on the dog. Some Labs are ready to hunt productively by the beginning of their first season, while others would be ruined by a premature introduction to the discipline necessary for even the most casual work in the field. The important point is to keep the training fun, and above all to subjugate your own immediate needs and expectations to the interest of the dog's long-term development.

Puppyhood, like childhood itself, is something that only happens once. While it

remains an important time in which to introduce the basic rules of socialization, enforcement of the rules should come as unobtrusively as possible, without compromising the sense of wonder on the part of any of the participants, human or canine.

If all goes well, puppyhood will end with more than a dog ready to begin training in earnest. It will end with an enduring emotional bond and it will mark the beginning of a friendship guaranteed to last for life.

And remember that in our own difficult day and age, a guarantee like that cannot be purchased at any price.

CHAPTER TWO

It's...Show time!

After the cute and cuddly phase of puppyhood, the adolescent Lab—loosely defined as a dog in its first two seasons—emerges as the haphazard sum of multiple parts: legs, nose, and heart, all fueled by an apparently limitless supply of enthusiasm. Brains, it should be noted, remain optional, although there will come a time for them later. Fortunately.

Like all teenagers, Labs in their first few seasons display more physical ability than judgment. Suddenly big and strong enough to go all day, they still lack the insight needed to keep their concentration focused on the task at hand, and they seem endlessly ready to substitute their canine *joie de vivre* for common sense. Reconciling this disparity, of course, falls to the trainer, and the Lab's adolescent years are, above all, a period of intense interaction between dog and handler.

Rising to that challenge requires its own measure of patience and the ability to see past immediate irritations to appreciate the dog's hidden potential. And there will be irritations. At this age, a playful leap can produce bruises on the part of its recipient, and the lingering puppyish urge to chew often produces results that mimic weapons of mass destruction. Adolescent Labs seem to relish asserting their

independence, often by forgetting overnight everything you've spent weeks patiently teaching them. But let's be honest. Didn't we do pretty much the same thing as teenagers?

At least Labs, in contrast to their human adolescent counterparts, come with built-in means of endearing themselves to those around them, no matter how trying they can occasionally become. For all their misplaced exuberance, young Labs positively radiate charm. No matter how much trouble they sometimes cause, they can always convince you that they never intended any harm, and their high jinks have a way of producing the kind of laughter that begs its own official pardon. Granted, this principle may be tested when the dog has just chewed up, say, the entire interior of a new pickup truck, but no one can pull off that kind of stunt and get away with it quite like a young Lab.

These are the years when each dog's individual personality begins to assert itself. Given their common genetic background, it's remarkable just how much variation in character Labs demonstrate, and the emergence of those traits during adolescence serves to remind even expe-

rienced trainers that they are dealing with true individuals, each as unique as the humans who surround them. After all the pheasants are flushed and all the ducks retrieved, it is those individual personality traits that linger in the human memory, and this is the time they begin

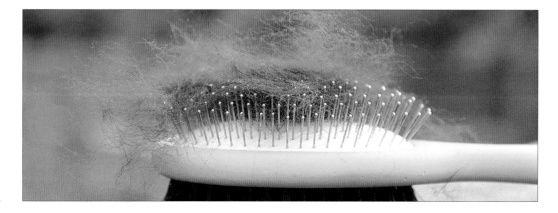

to emerge in earnest, to the delight and occasional consternation of all concerned.

The human bonding that began during puppyhood reaches its full expression during the dog's adolescent years. The dog's principal mission in life becomes simply to be with you and to please you once it's there. At first, it doesn't really matter what you're doing; focused enthusiasm for the hunt and related activities can wait until later. Running in the park, taking a bath, going for a ride to explore the world beyond the immediate confines of home … all are equally exciting to the young Lab, at least as long as you are there. This combination of enthusiasm and unqualified devotion can make up for a lot of youthful indiscretion on the dog's part, and while it's always dangerous to ascribe human characteristics to animals, it's hard to escape the feeling that they know it.

The second cardinal Labrador trait that reaches its full expression during the teenage years is the urge to retrieve. The instinct that looked cute and inspiring during puppyhood becomes—with luck—an obsession, and channeling that instinct into useful hunting qualities becomes the cornerstone of the interaction between dog and trainer. One cannot, after all, truly teach a dog to retrieve; one can only mold the retrieving instinct to one's own intentions. The finished product may not be ready for prime time until the end of adolescence—if at all—but it is the miracle of the dog's innate urge to fetch that sustains both trainer and charge during the challenging early phase of the learning process.

THE LIFE OF A LAB

What do young Labs want to fetch? As it turns out, just about anything. Training dummies may well be the specified objects of attention, but at this age Labs approach the retrieving game with catholic tastes. Hair brushes, shoes, Frisbees … virtually anything that will fit inside the dog's mouth (or close to it) can be fair game. Needless to say, these adolescent romps produce occasional misunderstandings. But even when you've spent an hour looking for a misplaced tennis shoe only to find it in the dog box, it pays to remember that the instinct is irreplaceable, and that the goal is to focus it rather than to extinguish it with a heavy hand.

During the teenage years, the Lab's inherent affinity for water reaches its full expression. If there is open water in the area (or even a good dose of wet mud), the young Lab will find it and practice its own canine form of total immersion. As always, the dog's manners may occasionally

run afoul of its enthusiasm. Bystanders should expect to be anointed without warning by shaking Labs, and muddy footprints have a habit of appearing where and when you least expect them. At times like this, it pays to remember that if you wanted a pet, you would have bought a poodle.

Sometime during this stage of development, the dog will make its crucial introduction to the real thing: birds with feathers. Whether this seminal moment comes courtesy of a pigeon in the back yard or a brace of mallards brought home with the help of an older dog, the youngster's view of the world will likely never be the same again. Granted, the dog's first impression may be difficult to gauge, with responses ranging from nervous sniffs to all-out assault. But most Labs sense at once that birds, as opposed to random objects and even training dummies, demand a

unique measure of attention, and that they are to be regarded with a form of respect reserved for birds and birds alone.

With all these elements in place, the adolescent Lab's training begins in earnest. The tempo of the process will vary according to both the dog's ability and the trainer's expectations, which may range from an occasional duck blind companion to a field trial champion. Whether the goal is a dog that will mark triples or simply sit on command, the principles are largely the same: Start slowly, build on what you have already established, and never forget that you are dealing with an individual. And no matter how slowly progress sometimes seems to come, remember that the Lab's cardinal personality trait—eagerness to please—always remains on your side.

THE LIFE OF A LAB

Some time during adolescence, the dog will earn the right to go on its first hunting trip. This is a big day for all concerned, and the occasion should be treated with all the ceremony it deserves. If you really need to bring home a limit of birds, it's best to hunt with a more experienced retriever. Wait until you can devote the hunt to the dog and do your best to make everything fun for your young charge, even if that means leaving the field prematurely. Expect sloppy manners in blinds and don't take along anything that can't stand a little bit of pond water. Give the dog time to explore its new surroundings, time to be a dog. The impressions made during that first glorious day afield may well last a lifetime.

No matter how well the training process appears to be going, adolescent Labs demonstrate a maddening tendency to regress to less mature behavior periodically and without warning. This kind of thing can make you wish you had bought a poodle, especially when you have bragged long and loud about the dog's performance, only to have it start eating ducks the first time you take it hunting with company. Patience, patience, patience! There will come a point when this sort of thing needs to be dealt with forcefully, but for the time being, remem-

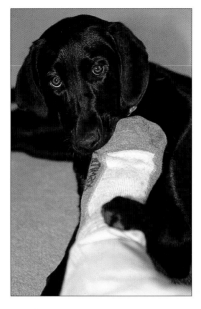

ber that what the dog craves most is your company and admiration. Quietly withdrawing what the dog wants more than anything can be a powerful motivator. "Time-Out" worked on us when we were kids, and guess what? It works on young Labs too.

In fact, the Lab's generic eagerness to please always lies at the heart of the training process. It is amazing how a dog that can tolerate so much when it comes to retrieving ducks from icy water can tolerate so little when it comes to human displeasure. The wise trainer never loses sight of this principle. Young dogs will inevitably rebel against authority, but they can only bluff so long. Temporarily deny them the feedback they crave and it's only a matter of time until the pleading looks and abject whines begin. Do you give in and readmit them to your company? Of course you do. But if you've played your cards right, your young charge will have learned something in the process, and may resist the temptation to misbehave the next time around. For a while, at least.

Adolescence, as no other time in a Lab's life, marks a period of transition. In the beginning, the dog is scarcely more than an overgrown puppy, all random energy and unfocused enthusiasm. At this stage of development, the young Lab can certainly be charming in a "Let's go for it!" kind of way, but the dog will scarcely be good for anything except companionship and occasional comic relief. By the end of adolescence, however, the youngster—with your help—will have learned a thing or two about life's responsibilities, including the need to conform some of that enthusiasm to your own wishes. And if you have really done your job well, by the end of your Lab's adolescence your expectations and the dog's will have become more or less inseparable.

The dog wants that to happen, and therein lies the essential miracle of the Labrador retriever.

CHAPTER THREE

The Mature Lab

At last! After all those years of puppy silliness and frustrating plateaus during the training process, the Lab has become something that approaches a finished product. That sense of completion is illusory, of course; Labs never finish their development any more than we do. Nonetheless, the period bounded approximately by the dog's third and eighth seasons represents a marvelous confluence of judgment and physical ability, a time when the dog knows what to do and maintains the physical skills needed to get the job done. While it's probably unfair to suggest that this is the happiest period in a Lab's life just because this is the time when the dog makes you the happiest, these years are certainly the most productive, whether you measure their output in terms of retrieved ducks or licked faces.

Physically, this is when Labs emerge as splendid canine athletes capable of working heavy cover all day long in pursuit of upland game and breaking your heart with their courage and tenacity in the water. Their special combination of endurance, strength, and heart can make even seasoned observers shake their heads in disbelief. In the field, they positively demand that game birds do what they want them to, never mind the thorns and brambles and long

THE LIFE OF A LAB

miles beneath the relentless autumn sun. Retrieves begin with unnecessary but utterly marvelous explosions. All that show and style may or may not result in more game in the bag at the end of the day, but it's guaranteed to remind you why you chose to hunt with a Lab.

All this athleticism reaches a culmination of sorts in the mature Lab's water entry. The term itself is something of a misnomer, for Labs this age don't just enter water, they positively attack it. Launched like cruise missiles, they seem to delight in extending their hang time and hitting the surface with as much commotion as possible, as if geysers of pond water were every bit as important as the retrieve. The higher the bank, the greater their enthusiasm for the upcoming splash, and truly frigid water only seems to encourage the performance. Do they do all this to show off, or simply to satisfy some inarticulate demand on the part of their own

THE LIFE OF A LAB

genetics? Who knows? But this kind of display serves to define the Labrador retriever at the height of its potential, and it stands as an experience that no admirer of the breed should miss.

Mentally, the dog's mature years are characterized by the ability to profit from its own experience. No amount of training can truly teach a dog to hunt. The best one can expect of the foundation laid during adolescence is the creation of an environment in which the dog

can teach itself. Wise handlers recognize that just as there is a time to intervene, there is also a time to let the dog explore the hunting experience on its own. This policy's rewards reach their full expression during the Lab's maturity. Dogs that once fidgeted hopelessly inside duck blinds suddenly begin to sit and scan the skies as patiently as their human companions do. Roosters that used to squirt away to safety in heavy cover now find themselves flushed within shotgun range by determined canine maneuvering. All these accomplishments stem from a quality that seemed hopelessly remote during the early years: wisdom.

The degree to which any dog can reason remains a matter of scientific debate. But what we're describing here isn't rocket science. Mature dogs — at least the good ones — simply learn with the passage of time that certain kinds of behavior produce certain kinds of results. And since grown Labs crave retrieves more than anything except your attention, they eventually modify their own behavior in order to produce them. While the basic formula of stimulus and response remains no more complicated than it was when the dog first learned the command "Sit," the ability to polish skills on one's own requires a certain measure of maturity just as surely as it remains a marvel to behold.

Emotionally, the mature Lab begins to act less like a social liability and more like an old friend. As in any relationship, including human marriage, sustained familiarity eventually produces a level of understanding impossible to duplicate in any other way. And so it goes between Lab and handler during the dog's mature years. Both parties learn not to sweat the small stuff. Dogs know when they can break a rule or two now and then just as you know when to let them. You forgive their occasional mistakes just as they forgive your occasional (let's hope) misses with the shotgun. Situations that once found you and the dog wrestling each other for control are now more likely to find you talking things over. And I do mean talking, in a language that goes far beyond the practical vocabulary of sit, come, stay, over, back. After all, that's what old friends are for, isn't it?

After a season or two of this kind of interaction, it becomes all too easy to sit back and enjoy the illusion of the finished product mentioned earlier. In fact, Labs come with a built-in tendency to regress, which can be a source of both devilment and charm. Beneath the surface of every well-mannered, "finished" Labrador lurks the soul of a puppy, and it often takes sur-

prisingly little encouragement for the puppy to emerge, often when least expected. The young dog's affinity for children, for example, never really goes away. Give a Lab some open space, a couple of kids, and a Frisbee, and it's only a matter of time until even the most seasoned campaigner starts carrying on as if it had never

heard a command in its life. And if there aren't any birds around to retrieve, creative Labs always stand ready to make do with a variety of substitutes, ranging from sticks to brook trout. Goofy as all this sometimes seems, it pays to remember that this is what you taught them. Sort of.

How the handler responds to these dalliances depends upon the expectations for the dog. Such carrying on is frowned upon in serious field trial circles, probably with some justification. But even well-trained hunting dogs deserve a measure of free expression. A formal workout or two with an old training dummy usually suffices to get the dog back in focus, and Labs should always be given an opportunity to be, well … Labs.

In biologic terms, the definition of maturity centers upon the ability to procreate. Because the dog's progression from puppy to adult takes place so quickly, this aspect of development can easily catch observers by surprise. When Labs decide to make more Labs, it's easy to wind up feeling like parents watching their cute little daughter climb onto the back of a Harley and blast off into the night with her arms wrapped around a bearded biker. This much always remains true: If it can happen, it will. During the Lab's mature years, those who picked male puppies from the litter box should expect all manner of wandering and generally lunatic behavior. Those who chose females should stand forewarned.

Planned breedings, of course, are another matter. Litters of puppies obviously remain essential to the enjoyment of Labrador retrievers. Male Labs make remarkably indifferent fathers, and they tend to view their offspring, if at all, as little more than unworthy rivals for human attention. Mature females, on the other hand, usually take to motherhood just as naturally as they take to water. Good thing; it's an important job, and someone has to treat it with the respect it deserves.

The dog's desire to share the activities of daily family life remains its primary social impulse, one that never diminishes. The puppy's wild enthusiasm may well mellow with age, but don't let the mature dog's apparent nonchalance fool you for a minute. Labs always love going places as long as they're going with you. Whether you're headed out to fish, jog, or shop, the dog will still spend hours waiting at the door just for the opportunity to tag along. Granted, none of these domestic activities may rival hunting in importance, but Labs never outgrow their capacity to appreciate the next best thing.

THE LIFE OF A LAB

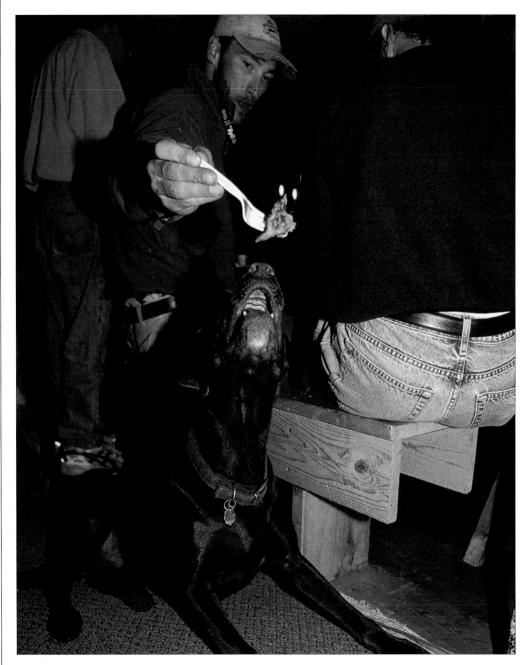

In fact, despite the high drama of long retrieves in icy water, the essential element of the mature Lab's contribution to the human lives that surround it boils down to one word: companionship. While the dog may be in the prime of its life as a hunter, the memories that endure are just as likely to focus on what takes place away from the field: moments shared, ears scratched, snacks stolen from the table. These are the experiences that enforce the distinction

between dogs as hunting machines and dogs as members of the family. And machines, let us remember, are objects to be purchased and maintained; family members only arrive by way of nurture. Of course, accepting a dog as a member of the family imposes its own share of demands, but the rewards are commensurate with the investment — not of money, but of time, patience, and understanding.

All this sounds very much like a definition of love, which is exactly as it should be.

CHAPTER FOUR

The Winter of Their Years

The signs appear subtly at first: a few insidious flecks of gray in the muzzle, a slow climb back into the kennel at the end of a long day afield, some stiffness in the same legs that once seemed all but immune to fatigue. But because the time scale of a Lab's life passes so quickly, it seldom takes long for the inevitable conclusion to sink in. The dog is growing old, and at least in physical terms, the peak performance years suddenly feel like history. This realization often seems easier on the dog than its human companions, but fortunately for all concerned, Labrador retrievers practically define the art of aging gracefully.

In fact, by canine standards, Labs usually remain remarkably hale and hearty well into the final years of their lives, and many of them continue to hunt enthusiastically at an age when representatives of other breeds are content to snooze away their days in front of the fireplace. Nonetheless, old age can be a period of difficult adjustment for both dog and handler, a time for thought and reflection as well as altered practical expectation. Managed properly, these years can provide unique insight into the Lab's remarkable character and produce some of the most irreplaceable memories from a lifetime's worth of canine companionship.

Aging Labs develop a wonderful economy of motion to compensate for the effects of all those long, hard miles on the chassis. The bounce of the younger days may be gone forever, but Labs never loose their enthusiasm for all the activities they enjoyed earlier in life. It may take them a bit longer to get from point A to point B, but they still maintain a remarkable capacity to get there, even if there is more shuffle and less spring to their gait. And older

Labs have a way of accepting these new limitations without complaint that should set an example for the rest of us as we eventually grow older ourselves.

While Labs may balk at the notion of retirement, they positively enjoy the opportunity their advancing years provide to reign supreme as canine characters. Secure in the conviction of their own worth, they tend to act like elder statesmen around the family, examining the goings-on of daily life with oddly serene detachment. If there is ever a suggestion of disdain in their attitude, they reserve it for the new pretenders in the kennel, dogs that everyone knows will never get the job done half as well as they once did themselves. Fortunately, they communicate such impressions nonverbally, or else we'd all have to endure long rounds of stories beginning with "Why, back when I was a puppy…"

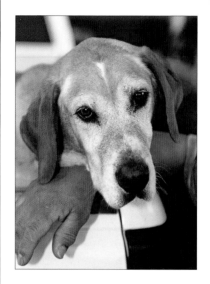

While Labs in their dotage sometimes act less demonstrative than they once did, they never outgrow their craving for human companionship. Why else would one leave the security of a warm fireplace to accompany you during even the most mundane daily activities? If anything, older dogs seem even less selective than their younger counterparts when it comes to the definition of adventure. Fetching a limit of ducks remains the gold standard, but if that option isn't available, a walk in the garden will certainly do.

Aging Labs tend to develop all sorts of odd household habits. Most of them eventually select a *querencia*, a randomly chosen resting spot they favor above all others, for reasons known only to the dog. Located at the foot of an old chair or the corner of a carpet, the dog always feels secure there and will predictably return to that precise spot after a trying day

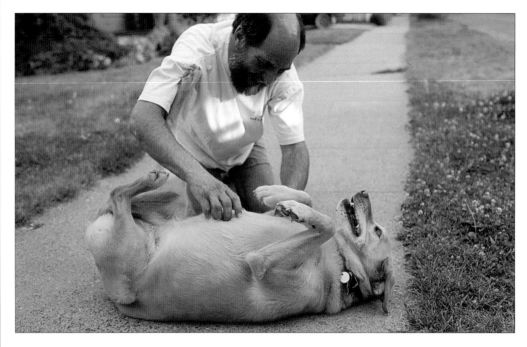

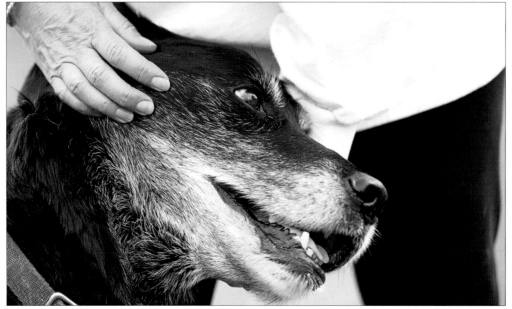

spent fetching ducks or, for that matter, doing nothing except growing old. They become remarkably sly about sneaking food treats, and to accomplish this mission they develop a repertoire of tricks that includes everything from charm to outright pilferage. And despite their occasional diffidence toward younger hunting dogs, they tend to make amends with cats and other household pets they once would have greeted with growls, sometimes even inviting these old adversaries to share their favorite spot on the rug. Will wonders never cease?

Of course, some of these lapses come at a cost to those who share the dog's world, especially its living space. From dog hair on the sofa to missing wieners from the grill, aging Labs never run out of ways to remind you that they no longer feel obligated to play by all those cumbersome old rules. But we always

find ways to forgive them their trespasses, out of respect for all that they have done for us and the ways they found to brighten our own lives over the years. And they never seem to run out of ways to enforce the case for understanding, from a heart-stopping retrieve when you thought you'd never see another one, to a wet, sloppy dog kiss just when the weight of the world seems to be collapsing on your own shoulders. And there never seems to be anything calculating about this behavior. They act this way because … well, because they're Labs.

In the field, Labs of this age display a refined caginess that can compensate for all kinds of dwindling physical resources. Relying on brains and noses rather than sheer animal drive, they

become consummate canine problem solvers. The solutions they come up with may not look conventional, but the dogs always seem to find a way to get the job done, even on legs that have clearly seen better days. Fallen birds may be able to run, but they'll have a hard time hiding from these seasoned veterans, not after all those years of on-the-job training. "Been there, done that" might well serve as the old Lab's motto when it comes time to work out a difficult retrieve, and those years of accumulated wisdom can make up for all kinds of physical shortcomings.

And no matter how weak the flesh becomes, the spirit always remains willing. The capacity of the older Lab to face challenges in the field with enthusiasm and courage never ceases to inspire, and sometimes it can positively break your heart. The widening gap between the dog's capabilities and its unflagging desire can pose a real dilemma for the handler, and some of the most difficult aspects of managing the older Lab in the field arise from indecision about just how much you should still let the dog do. While the idea of sending an old campaigner into freezing water or letting the dog work pheasants until it can't get back into the rig without a boost inevitably produces a certain level of discomfort, the alternative may be even worse. After all, leaving a dog behind can wound the spirit even more than the demands of the field, as you'll find out the first time you don your hunting clothes, grab your shotgun, and try to sneak out the door alone. Such piti-ful whines and wounded looks! Perhaps it's best in the end to listen to what the dog has to say. After all those years, your canine friend is certainly entitled to an opinion.

It makes sense to approach the problem with the same kind of subterfuge we use on our own children, by letting the dogs think they're doing more than they really are. Chose kinder, gentler patches of upland cover; take the old-timer duck hunting on warmer days. The idea is to create the illusion that nothing has changed, even though you know better. Chances are the dog does too. But if you have done your job well, the older Lab will be perfectly happy to join you in this willing suspension of disbelief as long as you provide an opportunity for a retrieve or two and effectively communicate the pleasure and satisfaction these performances provide.

THE LIFE OF A LAB

None of this should suggest that a day in the field with an older dog requires a patronizing attitude. In fact, the dog's experience and years of accumulated wisdom may well lead to some of the most memorable performances of its career. But even when it takes considerable effort to accomplish tasks once regarded as routine, the satisfaction often proves immeasurable. You will likely find yourself hunting for the dog's sake more and more, both for the pleasure of companionship and the importance of cramming as many of those experiences as possible into the seasons that remain.

The only predictable tragedy about our relationship with Labrador retrievers is that we will almost always outlive them. That's a matter of biology, the fate locked inside all our genes, and its conclusion stands as inevitable as our own mortality. And so there must eventually come a time for one last walk across the

grass, a final reminiscence about all that has transpired between you since that first introduction beneath the dam's watchful eye so long ago you cannot fathom how it manages to feel like yesterday. Then it is over, leaving behind an aching emptiness so much greater than the sum of its parts that it seems impossible to imagine that feeling of loss arising from nothing more than an old dog's absence.

But old Labs never die any more than old soldiers do. They live on in the spirit of new litters and new adventures to be shared by all who appreciate the breed and their ability to enrich our lives. And that is as it should be.

In fact, that is how the dogs themselves would want it.